Equip

God's

People

Present and Future Parish Training Schemes

by

Peter Lee

Rector of Christ Church, Addington, Durban
(Till July 1976 Assistant Curate, St. Paul's, Onslow Square, London, S.W.7)

GROVE BOOKS
BRAMCOTE NOTTS.

CONTENTS

EDITOR'S NOTE

Through Peter Lee's own movements this booklet had to go through the press whilst he was leaving England and taking up a new ministry in South Africa. He himself notes the enquiry had to be cut short (it did, for instance, hardly run beyond evangelical parishes initially, so that the Margaret Street 'Institute of Christian Studies' is not mentioned). In addition, most parishes gave their own accounts of themselves—and they remain unchecked. Finally, the editor must take responsibility for the particular abridging and presentation of the actual syllabuses (Peter Lee prefers the clumsy to the precious as the plural of syllabus!) in order to meet the pressures of space. The general air of the provisional and experimental is no accident, but an exact reflection of the parishes reported . . .

C.O.B.

THE QUESTIONNAIRE (see page 4)

The following questions were asked:

1. At what levels do you aim to teach your Christian group, e.g. new Christians; lay readers; other clergy; youth only; etc?
2. What patterns did you inherit from previous ministry in the place? How would you assess their past and present effectiveness?
3. What plans have you and your contemporary lay leaders initiated? Why? How would you assess their effectiveness?
4. What topics would you seek to cover, and what skills develop, at each level? (Please enclose any current literature you can, e.g. syllabus, study material, etc.).
5. How long do courses/sessions run, and how do they integrate into your overall church programmes?
6. Do any courses you have confine themselves to study, or are they integrated with worship and/or pastoral care and/or practical Christian service?

(The seventh question asked for the names of neighbours with interesting training schemes whom we could approach).

First Impression August 1976

ISSN 0305 3067

ISBN 0 901710 96 2

INTRODUCTION

The Christian Church has always been an educator, for two main reasons: for one it is supremely a body with a point of view, and it has wanted to instruct its members and persuade outsiders about this from the day of Pentecost onwards; for another it has cared about mankind and seen the provision of education as a basic humanitarian task. In a variety of ways (quite impossible to quantify) the church's educating role appears to have been eroded in recent decades. At one level the arrival of universal education run largely by secular authorities has meant, at the least, that there is no guarantee of even basic Christian learning being picked up at school, for the children of Christian families let alone others; but the churches, who used to run the schools and have therefore exported most of their teaching of the young to them, have been slow to fill the gap on their own premises and timetables. Perhaps more seriously, at the adult level serious training has tended to gravitate to the few who can stand in for the many (usually the clergy) rather than being seen as a continuing need and major priority for all Christians in responsible roles in the churches.

In recent years a fresh breath has been blowing around this area. On the positive side a fresh appreciation of the nature of the church has led to a desire for members of Christ's Body to mobilize their gifts, and this has brought its own desire for training of the gifts for useful service. The reverse and more cynical side of the same development has been the decline in full-time clergy and the need to equip people to fill some at least of their roles. The extent of this change in very recent time can be seen in the fact that around half the Grove Booklets published to date could be said to deal in various ways with this very issue.

The immediate origin of the present booklet was a discussion among some London church staffs in which everyone suddenly began to dream visions of the future in this field, in terms of making training resources and syllabuses available to groups around the country which they could work up into local schemes with local teachers, and maybe even have the whole thing nationally certificated by a central body such as (say) the Church of England Evangelical Council. More of this anon; it struck me that the first step was to find out what the present position is in some at least of our churches and to make some of the present schemes available to people who would quite like to run some kind of course in their own church but have never had the spare energy to construct one of their own.

Then too the first run of questionnaires went to a quite arbitrary list of places, and we asked for people's ideas for others to approach to make it less haphazard; this could only partially be done. When the replies came it was evident that some quotation would be valuable, but I had failed to ask for permission for this and have not been able to go back for it. I have therefore adopted the expedient of quoting fairly freely but only giving the source when it would help to have the context, and then only for strictly descriptive material. Opinions are given anonymously and I hope that contributors will find this compromise acceptable.

Peter Lee, July 1976

1. THE PROCEDURE

The survey on which I am reporting was hastily compiled and quite unscientifically conducted; nevertheless it yielded some interesting results.[1]

A first mailing of 80 brought 27 replies, three of which were apologies for being unable to help through pressure of work or too recent arrival in the parish. In the event the followup mailing only amounted to ten, but brought eight replies. There was a helpful supply of literature from assorted schemes as well as letters and returned questionnaires. In chapter 2 I will try to set out the present picture and some of the trends from what evidence I have. Chapter 3 describes some particular fresh initiatives which are taking place and contains a few syllabuses to inspire your own ideas; Chapter 4 will make a brief assessment and look forward.

It is worth noting at this point that there are the three main groupings of people for whom the kind of training schemes envisaged in the questionnaire (and explained in the covering letter asking for help) seemed inapplicable.

First were the overworked, for whom serious lay training seemed a good but unattainable vista of distant Sion; 'we tend to be governed by the pressure of things which have to be done' . . . 'your questionnaire is welcome, challenging and flattens a body to the wall!'

Second were the situations in which a traditional pattern of sermons, midweek Bible studies and pre-packed courses for Sunday School teachers appears to be adequate and effective; 'we have nothing more exciting than consecutive exposition at Sunday services. Whether because of this or in spite of it our congregation seems to produce Christian workers and leaders and soulwinners? . . . our neck of the woods is not one where whizz-kids breed in great numbers.' (Maidstone, Michael Wilcock). That, of course, is perfectly legitimate.

Thirdly came the expected comments of the churches in areas of non-middle class, non-cerebral or non-stable population. 'Your questionnaire is virtually unanswerable . . . we are still very much in the pioneering stage . . . So many Christian folk have left the area and we find ourselves in many ways back at square one on this particular issue' (Liverpool, Julian Charley). And from elsewhere: '[Courses etc.] presuppose a certain level of cerebral development in the faith which is beyond very many Christians in our industrial parishes. 22 years in this particular sphere of ministry have convinced me that syllabuses and courses are of little or no real value here. They have been tried—in connection with Billy Graham Crusades, Call to the North, etc.—but their impact has been minimal—yet! we have some fine Christian folk.'

Granted all this, we still have an obligation to equip Christians with as much understanding of their faith and as much usefulness in ministry as they can achieve; we still have greater opportunities and more hunger for learning than for many years; and we still have to prepare people to fill the huge manpower needs in the activities of the church of the future. How are we doing?

1 The text of the questions asked is set out on p.2 above.

2. THE PRESENT POSITION

(a) The levels taught

The first question was largely designed to test a double prejudice of my own, namely that an inordinate amount of effort goes into young people's teaching at the expense of evangelism and training among adults and whole families, and that most courses are graded according to physical age rather than to maturity in Christian faith.

Naturally enough, the churches in middle-class residential areas reflect their need to cater for the young. A run of Sunday School (just sometimes Children's Church—which is different), Climbers, Explorers, Pathfinders and Campaigners often leads in the general direction of a confirmation class with a youth fellowship of some kind as follow-up. This usually leads to an adult diet of Sunday services and sermons supplemented by midweek Bible studies in homes or centrally (or alternating).

It is the eclectic congregations in large cities, perhaps because they are less under pressure to cater for children, who tend to train people according to Christian maturity rather than physical age. For instance, All Souls, Langham Place, W.1. has till recently run four-weekly 'nursery' classes for new Christians and then training courses in basic doctrines and skills for adult members, as well as leadership training for potential leaders in addition. This last relates to an annual Training School leading to commissioning for work in the church's life, which has been effective and has held people's commitment while having the less fortunate effect of letting the non-commissioned feel that much less useful. The opening of the new plant at All Souls coincides with the appointment of a director of training full-time to the staff, so the whole area of training is being seen as central to the contribution which an eclectic fellowship can make in preparing people for a role in the churches in which they are later to settle.

Increasingly a person's potential for useful service is becoming the criterion for his inclusion in training. Most of the newest courses are connected to some activity in which it is hoped the members will engage together, most commonly home visiting (with the frequent mention of Evangelism Explosion, and the equally frequent and emphatic comment, *'much amended'*). Also included are courses in leading home groups or Bible studies (we recently had 65 clients in St. Paul's, Onslow Square alone for one of these, from a realistic membership of only 300 or so).

A surprising number of churches run their own home-built Readers' courses, and there is a welcome growth in 'pastoral care courses'. John Baker describes the following pattern he earlier knew at Gillingham:

(a) A basic 'pastoral care' course for lay men and women (6 weeks)
(b) A basic course for potential 'teachers' at all levels (6 weeks)
(c) A basic course in evangelism (mainly personal, but including house-groups etc) (6 weeks)
(d) A more advanced course in pastoral care, including healing and ministry to people with deeper problems (9 weeks)

All in all, it seems that the human and published resources for teaching children and teenagers are still there where they are needed, and only the local church can tell whether the amount of human resources committed there are disproportionate. Some churches are well organized for the adult convert but many are not, unless by good chance their house groups or confirmation classes catch the intake adequately. On the other hand the training of workers is receiving a high priority and is at least engaging plenty of thought—though Gordon Jones in Orpington is alone in contributing a course on being an effective member of the P.C.C. The non-Christian is in mind both in evangelistic training for Christians, and in open groups for thought and discussion; Christ Church, Clifton, Bristol reports a six-week training programme 'for those seeking to become Christians, to think out the Christian faith and perhaps to be confirmed.' This is a free and easy discussion group, but it has structure through a duplicated agenda of subjects and weekly notes for thought and study.

(b) The patterns adopted

It is difficult to see what training within any actual church fellowship feels like, without experiencing the life of that particular fellowship, from the inside, but the second and third questions were designed to elicit, not only the current shape of things in the life of the churches, but to see what changes had been felt necessary and the needs and priorities whch had prompted them. Here it is not easy to generalize beyond the healthy lack of complacency about inherited patterns (comments ranged from 'a bit traditional' and 'useless' to 'I have been here for 17 years so the question is not applicable'!).

For most contributors the inherited pattern consisted mainly of Sunday services with a straightforward sermon, usually backed by a midweek Bible study (often held centrally and, one suspects, in practice a mini-Sunday service with a longer exposition from the Vicar). To supplement this would be 'organizations'—that is, largely like-aged and like-minded people meeting in isolation to do their own things (nothing, of course, *necessarily* wrong with that).

The main shifts in pattern might be summarized as follows:

1. Use of Sunday: Here the eclectic fellowships are the most traditional, and perhaps rightly as they draw the kind of people who can gain from a fairly sustained cerebral presentation from the pulpit. This is seen very positively: 'we have a 90% eclectic congregation, so Sunday Sermons (sic) have an importance for very many'. Others, however, are experimenting with the shape of worship to increase its educational effectiveness. Even Maidstone (where, you recall, the whizz-kids do not breed) reports revealingly: 'For what it's worth, our expository courses usually take us through a book of Scripture at a time, divided into (say) twenty sermons. Each sermon is accompanied by duplicated notes, integrated with the rest of the worship service (indeed, in the mornings it's *followed* by the worship, so that hymns/readings/psalms/prayers all underline the message), and by some of our house-groups used as a basis for discussion and prayer during the week following. It seems again and again to coincide remarkably with current pastoral and practical needs. I don't do twenty weeks in a row, of course—perhaps four or five at a time . . .'

Another similar and perhaps further development is worth quoting extensively, from St John's, Harborne in Birmingham: 'We see the family as an important unit, and want to encourage all-age worship together; it could be that our morning service will more and more centre on *all-age learning together* [my italics], in the context of Family Worship, and our evenings centre more on the relaxed enjoyment of worship, focussed in Holy Communion. In the mornings we plan to have a time of worship together (using M.P. Series 3) and then breaking into groups ranging from adults (prayer/hymn/sermon) to different age groupings (prayer/choruses/ activities/stories/group work etc.) It looks as though our easiest plan (at present) is to use the material at present used by our afternoon Sunday School, viz. Scripture Union; and with the help of their recent *In Touch* publication, we try to focus the worship into an integrated theme. In due course we can see that it may be right to produce our own syllabus, and teaching materials, and some work has been started on that.' There, incidentally, is an interesting example of a church grappling with the two scales of maturity, (crudely) physical age and spiritual understanding.

Other inherited forms also (such as confirmation classes) often now have the structure retained but the ingredients altered and shuffled.

2. Home groups: These have been a feature of church life for many years, but there is a marked shift of emphasis towards them in many replies. This is true even where the previous pattern is deeply respected, and very often shows up as a breakdown of the midweek central Bible study on at least some weeks of the month. Some do, and some do not, continue to dictate the agenda centrally; for some it would be impossible because they are deliberately using the midweek groups to divide people up according to the maturity of their understanding. Two fairly typical responses:

A. *Previous pattern:* 'Sunday sermon ministry basically. It gathered an eclectic congregation and certainly fed people.'
Present pattern: 'Strengthened the "Home Bible Group" concept—got 15 groups going—more informality needed: also, more of the fellowship that goes across "organizations"—more of the "family of God" idea. Also got a beginners group going.'

B. *Previous pattern:* 'Regular mid-week Prayer Meeting and Bible Study'.
Present pattern: 'Regrouping of mid-week Bible Study into two House Meetings, again with regular patterns of studies, either set books, or particular courses. One is geared for simplicity of approach, the other is more advanced, and sub-divides into two groups in the one house.'

Another variation on the theme is to run varied study groups in one building, but still to worship together as introduction or conclusion. 'I inherited a weekly Bible Study on a Wednesday evening, this has been changed so that on Wednesday evenings in term-time there is a Group Bible Study, the Course in Christian Studies, and a course for new Christians, taking place at the same time in different rooms in the Church, lasting one hour. We then all come together for prayer.' (Leeds, Michael Botting).

3. Lay involvement: This nearly goes without saying in the light of the activities described above, which could only survive with well-spread leadership. Nevertheless, it is a feature in practice all the way from Holy Trinity, Platt Lane, Manchester, who report a new pastoral eldership team of nine and the use of lay people in leading worship, to Holy Trinity, Eastbourne. Here a very effective role has come to lay people in leading the holidaymakers' epilogue service at 8.15 p.m. in summer, for which they have been inviting people during the day. Some contributors still sound a little surprised at how well it all seems to be going . . .

4. The nature of the church: Here, quite explicitly, is a theological key to much of the above. There is frequent mention of relationships between Christians, the support offered by close groups, the Body of Christ, gifts for service, etc. (Is this chicken or egg with the treatment of such subjects in several previous Grove Booklets?!) One example will make the point:

> *Previous pattern:* 'Confirmation course based on J. Stott's *Your Confirmation.* Usefully covers the ground, if a bit "traditional".'
> *Present pattern:* 'An increased emphasis on the Church, what it is, and what it means to belong, because, while the vertical relationship with God is adequately covered, the horizontal relationship . . . is weak.'

5. Planning: An interesting and encouraging sign is that, where previous patterns appeared quite haphazard with often many activities happening under the general umbrella of one church, there is now a sense in many places of the whole church's life being co-ordinated and thought through so as to move steadily forward together. What is more, this is rarely a blueprint of the incumbent's but more usually a joint plan prayed through and worked out by several responsible elder-figures together (either as, or with, the P.C.C.). Two examples follow, the first from a large suburban church:
'The parish has quite a lot of teaching opportunities which are carried on mainly in the context of each separate organization. We are now planning to have co-ordinated teaching sessions so that different youth organizations for example receive training together as well as in their specialized groups . . . There is a great need for helpful training which is organized for almost all and sundry . . . I see a need for Christian Essentials teaching groups which could perhaps cater for varying levels of need e.g. Lay Leaders, new Christians, refresher courses for stale Christians and more advanced training for the mature.' It would be fascinating to know how much of this shift from neatly segregated organizations to an all-in approach reflects new theological insight, how much the sociological effect of living in a less structured society, and how much simple retrenchment.

Another encouraging example shows what can happen when an under-used laity begins to grow in training and responsibility:

> *Previous pattern:* 'None'.
> *Present pattern:*
> '(1) Regular in-service training for all Sunday School and Pathfinder leaders etc. Training was important to begin with and proved so valuable that we made it a feature of every leaders' meeting.
> (2) Bible study/group leaders started to promote lay pastoral ministry: v. effective in giving skill and confidence.
> (3) General parish course in evangelism/outreach in preparation for diocesan year of mission. Quite effective in awakening concern.
> (4) P.C.C. study days: in worship, liturgy etc. to deal with current issues in church life.'

All this suggests that in some situations churches have been revising their strategy to meet the new situations which face us; even more encouragingly, others begin to think strategically instead of living hand-to-mouth.

(c) The topics covered

I want to leave any detailed listing of syllabuses to chapter 3 so that they are conveniently grouped together for reference. In general terms the answers to the fourth question (on topics and skills) ran as follows:

Basics: Many churches run some kind of course for new Christians, sometimes under the guise of Confirmation preparation, and this covers in most cases the elements of Christian belief, behaviour and church membership. This can then grow in various directions.

Bible: Again this is a fairly predictable area in evangelical churches, but the thoroughness and freshness of approach in some places are impressive. This relates to series of sermons for Sundays and good titles for them, but also to the way in which notes and outlines are produced for Sunday sermons and for midweek groups to use. Where more serious courses are attempted there is a welcome refusal to duck issues of historical background or the status of the Bible. The level of thought and apologetic which crops up as almost run-of-the-mill in some churches is evidenced in a series of fortnightly central studies at Emmanuel, Northwood (alternating with home group studies in Luke 24 and Acts 1 and 2):

God Speaks (the nature of Revelation)
Man Reasons (contemporary views)
The Spirit Breathes (the concept of Inspiration)
The Church Decides (the Canon of Scripture)
Archaeology Confirms (the evidence from archaeology)
The Christian Interprets (principles of hermeneutics)

Doctrine: Both in the more old-fashioned series of lectures which used to be available on weeknights in some churches (and were a splendid outlet for GOE notes!), and in the more ambitious modern schemes, there is quite a heavy and systematic treatment of doctrine in familiar, if formidable-sounding, categories to many people's ears: Inspiration, God, Man, Sin, Salvation, Eschatology, etc . . . But the same material comes across in a more digestible format in (for example) the CPAS training kits inspired by Gordon Jones, with tapes, filmstrips, and guides for group discussion.

Project-centred: Clearly much of the training outlined above has practical objectives which tend to dictate the content of the courses planned for them. Thus the Evangelism Explosion Visitation courses and various others from the Navigators, CPAS, or diocesan sources are in use in training people for home visiting, Lay Readership, outdoor evangelism, and the like. There is a heartening emphasis on apologetics, at the popular as well as the more cerebral level, as a back-up to schemes for evangelism in which workers might otherwise be skittled by the first question or objection they had to face on the doorstep.

Current affairs: Naturally many churches continue what, in our context at St. Paul's, we tend to call 'a walking Christian magazine', that is a get-together (often in the Sunday evening after-church slot) in which issues of current concern to Christians are dealt with. This includes overseas information and visits from missionaries, debates over moral issues, films, questions on controversial sermons, and so on; an attempt, in short, to keep Christians literate about events and arguments in which they are or ought to be involved.

(d) The integration of training into church life

The fifth question on the questionnaire had asked about the duration of courses and their integration into the church programme; and the sixth had been related, asking about the integration of training generally with worship and/or pastoral care and/or practical Christian service.

Apart from the observation that training goes on for ever, most churches seemed to favour courses ranging from just two or three sessions ('short and snappy') on a particular subject (such as leading group Bible study) through (most popularly) six or seven up to ten or so. Some naturally went in for two 'terms', one before and one after Christmas. There was a consensus that interest lags over a longer stretch and people want to know in advance how far ahead their diaries are committed—especially in churches where a certain night is not automatically earmarked. Of course a fortnightly series of seven, alternating with house groups or what have you, takes most of us nicely from Harvest to Advent, Christmas to Lent, or Easter to the summer holidays! Places with midday services during the week for businessmen or the like would not usually attempt more than four at a go. None of this really applies to the more ambitious courses, but even these tends to subdivide into 'terms', or sections of a few weeks.

As for individual sessions, most were agreed that 30-45 minutes was ample for the straight 'lecture' style, but that evenings involving a variety with discussion, role-play, group work, etc. could cheerfully run for a couple of hours even after a day's work. The School of Christian Studies takes people from work into a lecture, then a meal, then a second session. On the broader question of integration into the worship, care and action of the whole fellowship, two broad responses came back. On the action end one reply can speak for many: 'We are wholly committed to "on the job" training and believe it is a longstanding weakness of evangelicals to teach but not to "do".' This ties up with the emphasis, already noted, on training with a specific task in mind, and is found fairly commonly. All Souls Langham Place used to couple one study subject in an evening with one more practical subject, 'sometimes in Action'. A scheme in Southsea for young people, described more fully below, coupled intake of knowledge with output in Sunday School teaching. The same is naturally true of diocesan-based schemes for Readers or Auxiliary Pastoral Ministry. At parish level the two areas of greatest integration into action are evangelism (and related visiting) and the pastoral care by 'area elders' or the like.

The other broad response concerned house groups. These are increasingly seen as more than just Bible study groups. In particular the traditional 'time of prayer at the end' is seen as a time for worship and praise, often with music, as well as routine requests; and the pastoral care offered both by the host or leader and by the group as such among themselves is seen as vital. Again it would be nice to know just what this is reacting to—a fresh theology of the Body, a growth of personal needs in a tense society, or the simple shrinkage of clergy? In any event the growth, membership and supervision of home groups is clearly on the agenda of almost every church we approached, as being significant in helping the individuals they handled in their Christian growth: 'we try to feed new people into the group that is going to be most helpful to them at any particular stage'. We note a fear lest groups let some people 'coast' without commitment.

3. SOME FRESH INITIATIVES

General

It will be evident that there are several fresh initiatives under way, and that they lean in certain particular directions: the setting of specific goals, the richer use of homes, the stress on action. One realistic contributor underlines the well-earthed nature of the current mood: 'Previous teaching tended to be "inspirational" and it produced a high level of commitment but a lack of "theological" thinking (in broadest sense) and of the relationship of the faith to the world as it is—social, cultural, political aspects.' The main aim of this section is to describe how some of these hard-headed schemes are being tried in practice, and to offer their specific syllabuses as a kind of quarry from which others may be glad to mine ideas. The examples chosen are fairly typical of the thinking in many of the responses I received, though they have had the chance to work things out in more concrete detail—and of course there remains the question of how typical the whole sample was of the country's churches at large. They are typical in one or two specific senses: they are often reviewing and reviving some of the inherited patterns and giving them a dramatic facelift, they are usually keeping their eyes well open for new resources of every kind, and they are trying to grapple with some of the immediate pressures which easily cause others to take fright and dive for cover.

Taking the evangelistic opportunities

1. Christ Church Clifton was mentioned above as carrying a 'six week training programme for those seeking to become Christians, to think out the Christian faith and perhaps to be confirmed'. Each week there is a duplicated set of notes, of which a summary follows:

CHRISTIAN BASICS

Week 1 FINDING GOD THROUGH JESUS CHRIST

THE EVIDENCE THAT THERE IS A GOD—The way the world is made, the nature of man, limitations of this approach, probabilities.
WHO FINDS WHOM?—Man will never find God on his own.
GOD'S SEARCH FOR MAN—By messengers, then by his Son.
WHAT JESUS CHRIST ACHIEVED—Incarnation, ministry, death, resurrection.
THE EVIDENCE FOR JESUS' RESURRECTION—Empty tomb, changed disciples, etc.
WAS JESUS JUST A MAN OR WAS HE GOD?—His claims.
HOW DOES CHRIST ENABLE US TO FIND GOD TO-DAY?—Promise to be with his followers.

Week 2. THE HOLY SPIRIT AND LIFE AFTER DEATH

THE TRINITY—Definition, evidence, implications.
THE HOLY SPIRIT—His role on earth, his presence in all Christians.
THE CHRISTIANS' HOPE FOR THE FUTURE—Jesus' return, heaven, life after death.

Week 3. HOW TO BECOME A CHRISTIAN AND BE CERTAIN OF IT

FIRST STAGE—God speaks to us
SECOND STAGE—Our response .
A DEFINITE AND PUBLIC RESPONSE.
A CONTINUING RESPONSE—In context of Christian fellowship.
HOW CAN WE BE SURE WE ARE CHRISTIANS?—Trusting God's promise.

Week 4. THE KIND OF LIFE JESUS EXPECTS FROM HIS DISCIPLES

STANDARDS DO NOT MAKE YOU A CHRISTIAN—Necessary after becoming Christian.

THE TEN COMMANDMENTS—A good summary still, set out in full.

CHRIST'S COMMANDS TO US—Sermon on Mount, Jesus as perfect example, our need of God's strength.

WHAT JESUS CHRIST EXPECTS FROM US—Romans 12.

POINTS TO REMEMBER—Every Christian is useful, every chore involves living for Christ, lives witness as much as words, let Jesus direct us.

Week 5. THE HELP GOD PROVIDES TO LIVE THE CHRISTIAN LIFE—1

CHRISTIAN FELLOWSHIP—We need each other, must love each other, should share fellowship, encouragement, work.

PRAYER—Difficulties answered, teaching of Jesus, categories of worship/confession/thanks/intercession, four ways to pray.

THE BIBLE—Its trustworthiness, how to study it, attitudes when reading it, handling problems in its.

Week 6. THE HELP GOD PROVIDES TO LIVE THE CHRISTIAN LIFE—2

HOLY COMMUNION—Remembrance of Jesus, the Last Supper, Jesus' purpose in the institution, approaches to God in Communion, titles and patterns of the service.

[*This last set of notes ends with a tear-off slip to be sent to the Vicarage, asking for confirmation/Bible study notes/membership of Electoral Roll/delivery of parish news-sheet/joining a House Group*].

2. Holy Trinity Eastbourne is an example of a church prepared to undertake the twin-pronged task of reaching the resident neighbours as well as a seasonal influx of visitors. To describe the latter first (as it appears longer established), the main thrust is a Sunday evening epilogue service at 8.15 p.m. with invitations distributed beforehand to visitors to the town. The key is careful planning and preparation; the leader is expected to time the service for just 30 minutes, to choose the material and to co-ordinate the whole. Singers and preacher are carefully briefed and teams of 'fishers' to do the inviting are equipped with invitations and advised about the best times and places to go over the weekend. The clergy guide and supervise but the laity seem to do it all. It is not quite clear whether training in answering questions or in personal evangelism is given, or whether training for this work will in future be linked in with schemes for training the visitors of the local residential area. This local initiative arose from a synod report on evangelism and training in November 1975. An evangelism committee was formed with a view to training lay visitors to follow up existing contracts in the locality and to make new contacts with the residents of large blocks of flats near the church. They ran a pioneer scheme for six successive Thursdays with preliminary training, aiming to visit a spread of different kinds of people (married and single, varied ages, known to church and not) and then review the results. There was to be an introductory letter from the Vicar (personally signed) and only positive replies would be visited. Again the key was care and thoroughness—in drafting the letter, choosing the visitors, praying ahead and following up the visits conscientiously. They were also careful to send twos to visit single people, to decide who should be spokesman on each visit, and so forth. In addition they gave time to making their own modifications of the outline offered by Evangelism Explosion so that the questions asked in visiting came naturally to those using them. A series of lay training evenings had been laid on at deanery level with the Rev. Cyril Bridgland who has used Evangelism Explosion extensively at Holy Trinity Redhill; but the significant feature of Eastbourne's initiative is that they ran the pioneer scheme onto the beginning of his training sessions so that they already had some experience and momentum to contribute when the training began. This only began in 1976 so no reflections were available.

Tailoring training to church life

1. St. George's Leeds is one example of a church which has tried to introduce an ambitious scheme of Christian studies at the cerebral level while still holding this training firmly in the context of the life and work of a worshipping church. Here is their introduction and syllabus for the St. George's Course in Christian Studies:

INTRODUCTION

In these days of conflicting ideas it is essential for Christians to know what they believe and why. It is for this reason that this three-year cycle of Christian Doctrine, Ethics and Church History is being given at St. George's, Leeds.
The nine terms are being arranged to coincide with University terms to encourage students while in Leeds to equip themselves for future Christian service. As the terms constitute a cycle it is possible to begin at any term although regular attendance is essential if the full benefit is to be obtained.
Duplicated notes will be provided at each lecture.
The subjects being dealt with in the three shorter terms on Christian Ethics are deliberately not listed below as it is intended that they will deal with problems current at the time.
Most of the lectures will be given by St. George's staff but visitors will be invited to give some of the lectures.
The course is open to any who are interested and is not restricted to members of St. George's.

SYLLABUS

1. Autumn Term 1973. The Doctrine of Scripture, God, Man and Sin
[*8 headings are given covering these doctrines*]

2. Spring Term 1974. The History of the Church to 451 A.D.
[*8 headings are given including O.T. history as well as the N.T. and later periods*]

3. Summer Term 1974. Christian Ethics 4 sessions on current ethical problems

4. Autumn Term 1974. The Doctrine of Christ
[*8 headings are given on the cedal assertions*]

5. Spring Term 1975. The History of the Church from the Middle Ages to the present day
[*8 headings are given on the outstanding periods*]

6. Summer Term 1975. Christian Ethics 4 sessions on current ethical problems

7. Autumn Term 1975. The Doctrines of the Holy Spirit and Salvation
[*8 headings are given*]

8. Spring Term 1976. The Doctrines of the Church and Eschatology
[*8 headings are given including treatment of the sacraments*]

9. Summer Term 1976. Christian Ethics 4 sessions on current ethical problems

Michael Botting's response to the questionnaire should be read to set this in context. He describes All-age Instruction (for which see Grove Booklet 31) alongside the Course in Christian Studies, as well as a Lay Readers' Course in which about 10 are currently engaged. On Wednesday evenings the Course runs alongside group Bible Study and a course for new Christians with joint prayer at the end. Pastorally, they have developed lay elders responsible for the geographical area in which they live as regards leading Bible studies and laying on evangelistic outreach among friends. The leaders meet jointly with the staff quarterly, and occasionally share a weekend conference—as for example recently on pastoral counselling. On top of this there is a Sunday evening discussion get-together of the 'walking magazine' variety, and again there are thoughts of introducing something on the lines of Evangelism Explosion. So that, while the Course in Christian Studies is clearly a department of its own, is fairly academic and makes a point of being run when students are in term, every effort is made to keep open the contacts with worship together, with care for the individuals, and with a sense of practical responsibility on Christian service. Only the locals could tell us if it works or whether despite all this it becomes a cerebral ghetto.

2. St. Jude's Southsea are about to be quoted with apologies to the present leaders because of a scheme evolved there in 1962 for the Young Churchmen's Fellowship with the previous incumbent, the Rev. Don Churchman. This is quoted because it combines a thoroughly systematic scheme with a sharp awareness of the limits imposed by normal parish life. It is a scheme for the immediately post-Pathfinder generation who would therefore be around 15½ years old and would, in that situation, be mostly recently confirmed and currently engaged in 'O' levels. The course is designed for one year and aims to make allowances for such variables as pressure of school work, teenage goodwill, and the date of Easter.

The preamble explains that a Sunday morning slot can be claimed for the course which will catch the minds at their best while giving the course a certain importance in the eyes of members too. Because of the pressure of school work any 'homework' must be restricted and most of the learning must be self-contained; any projects for the holidays or weekends must also be realistic in scale. A wise remark from Derek Tasker's *Training the Youth Group* is quoted—'Many a young person has been temporarily or permanently lost to the Church through an over-employment of their good intentions at an early age.'

As for the teaching itself, it should seek to meet the three needs of training, fellowship, and counsel or direction, in a group setting. 'The best training is done within a fellowship—e.g. through guided discussion and corporate projects—so that the members, by *doing* (not just talking) together, in a sense train themselves and naturally create a closer fellowship, in which they become ready to share experiences and problems.' Every theme is pursued through discussion, visits and projects as well as formal talks, and a kind of dignity again imparted by using folders with duplicated inserts and charging a modest fee. Some kind of public 'commissioning' for a role in the church might climax the course, whether this is for Sunday School work (towards which the course leans) or other roles which could be developed as a positive means of using the young people's commitment. Apparent omissions from the syllabus are envisaged as being covered in the parallel Sunday evening Y.C.F. programme, e.g. prayer, overseas, family and sex, etc. The syllabus itself contains a self-contained Sunday School course which was not provided (try Don Churchman?). Here is the outline:

AUTUMN TERM (15 weeks)

Week 1 (a) Introduction to course
(b) Introduce idea of 'service'
(c) KNOW YOUR PARISH I—Area
2 KNOW YOUR PARISH II—Administration and organisations
3 ENJOY YOUR BIBLE I—Analysis of O.T. and N.T.
4 ENJOY YOUR BIBLE II—Bible geography
5 ENJOY YOUR BIBLE III—Bible history (intro.)

Weeks 6-14 Sunday School course, including visits to Primary and Junior Sunday School and report-back to discuss findings on prepared questions . . .
Week 15 Visit to a Free Church service (again with briefing plus report-back).
Other visits: Y.C.F. London Rally, Diocesan Conference, P.C.C. meeting
Projects included manual jobs in Youth Centre and 'Youth Page' in Parish Magazine.

SPRING TERM (12-16 weeks)

Week 1 KNOW YOUR CHURCH I—Deanery and diocese
2 KNOW YOUR CHURCH II—Convocation and Church Assembly
3 KNOW YOUR CHURCH III—Visit to an Anglo-Catholic service
4 ENJOY YOUR BIBLE IV—History of Israel I
5 ENJOY YOUR BIBLE V—History of Israel II
6 ENJOY YOUR BIBLE VI—Background to N.T. I
7 ENJOY YOUR BIBLE VII—Background to N.T. II

Weeks 8-16 Sunday School course as above
Other visits: British Museum (Biblical antiquities), Convocation, Synagogue.
Projects: Houseparty, visits, making models for S.S., publicity on missionary project, etc.

SUMMER TERM (12-16 weeks)

Week 1 ENJOY YOUR BIBLE VIII—Book
2 ENJOY YOUR BIBLE IX—Chapter
3 ENJOY YOUR BIBLE X—Verse
4 ENJOY YOUR BIBLE XI—Devotional reading

Weeks 5-9 Sunday School course in practice, learning on the job.
Weeks 10, 11 refresher and discussion of past five weeks in Sunday School teaching.
Week 12 *BOOKS*—a course bibliography and ideas for building a basic library.
Other visits: Choir practice, Baptism, Wedding, maybe a second P.C.C. meeting.
Projects in term: Collecting in Christian Aid Week, Youth Service, clean church.
Projects for summer holidays: Y.C.F. houseparty, work camp, outings for spastics, etc.

These last two terms are flexible according to the date of Easter.

We hardly do justice to the course by presenting it in this way; every week's subject is bracketed with suggestions as to how it should be taught and the available visual aids, duplicated sheets, and other resources which could be brought into play. By now of course it shows signs of age, if only because half the church institutions it mentions have been laid to rest, but the overall conception and approach, brought up to date, could very well be run more widely. For the leaders' benefit the course itself, including explanatory preamble, bibliography, and Y.C.F. constitution are bound in one efficient folder; as noted elsewhere, care and thoroughness are not optional handmaids to pastoral training. Quite apart from anything else, it saves endless time if you want to re-use a course—this one evidently ran with great effectiveness for ten years.

Using the resources

1. Christ Church Orpington is the latest beneficiary of Gordon Jones' attention, and shows up the way in which some of the newer educational media can be harnessed to routine parish life. He has, of course, been heavily involved in the production of the Group Learning Kits by CPAS. Some of their methods reappear in his parish; for example, he offers leaders of house groups a short introduction to the week's theme for study on cassette, especially when all groups are following a course which covers both central and home gatherings. We reproduce a recent programme for their confirmation course because it shows how the Group Learning Courses can be dovetailed into the calendar of the local church and can carry on into follow-up beyond confirmation itself.

CONFIRMATION COURSE (Tuesday, 7.30, unless stated, for approx. 1 hour)

March 18th	What is Confirmation?
March 27th	Maundy Thursday Communion (in Church).
April 1st	*UNDERSTANDING THE FACTS—MAN:* Sin, Suffering, Repentance, New Birth.
April 8th	*UNDERSTANDING THE FACTS—GOD:* His Character, His Work, God the Holy Trinity (wall chart).
April 14th	*(Monday) UNDERSTANDING THE FACTS—JESUS CHRIST:* Justification by faith, The Law of God, The satisfaction the Law demands, The satisfaction God provides, Pardon—Faith—Peace.
April 22nd	*UNDERSTANDING THE FACTS—HOLY SPIRIT:* Sanctification and the Holy Spirit, Prayer and the Holy Spirit, The Bible and the Holy Spirit The. Church and the Holy Spirit.
April 29th	Review Week.
May 6th	*ACCEPTING MEMBERSHIP—THE CHURCH:* The Church Spiritual, The Church Visible—Strategy and Structure.
May 13th	*ACCEPTING MEMBERSHIP—THE SACRAMENTS:* Baptism—Holy Communion (The Institution), Series 3 Service and reception.
May 20th	*ACCEPTING MEMBERSHIP—THE BIBLE:* Authority and Inspiration (wall chart), Use and study.
May 27th	*ACCEPTING MEMBERSHIP—PRAYER:* Corporate Worship and Prayer, Private Prayer and Rule of Life.
June 3rd	Review Week and Preparation for Confirmation on June 8th.
June 10th	Fellowship Evening—Celebration.
June 17th	*LEARNING FOR LIFE—CHRISTIAN MATURITY:* Spiritual Growth, The practice of the Gifts of the Spirit.
June 24th	*LEARNING FOR LIFE—FAMILY AND HOME:* Christian approach to marriage, Family relationships, The Christian home.
July 1st	*LEARNING FOR LIFE—WORK AND MONEY:* The Christian approach to Money (Possessions and Standards), attitude to Work and Ambition.
July 8th	*LEARNING FOR LIFE—CHRISTIAN SERVICE:* The Christian commitment to a life of service, Giving—Money—Time—Talents, Consideration of full-time Ministry.
July 15th	Fellowship Evening.

2. SS. Philip and Jacob Bistol ('Pip 'n Jay') may be thought to have their own ideas about resources; they publish their own leaflet on money, run an extensive tape library, and were the only contributor to mention a prayer school in their training programme. In many ways life is conventional; a midweek central Bible study alternating between exposition and subjects, confirmation classes every year or two, missionary conventions twice a year, and an annual houseparty with an imported speaker. Like others they are giving special attention to lay leaders, giving them their own weekend away annually, laying on specialist training sessions in counselling from time to time, and drawing together the Lay Readers every other month to practise and criticise service leading and preaching. Teaching is very much the midweek activity and 'Sunday is outreach and therefore evangelistic.' They gain a mention here as taking seriously the availability of very obvious media which others of us could use better. There are several homegrown leaflets, short and to the point, such as 'Giving is good for you!' (on money) and 'Sex is for loving'. These may seem unremarkable until one realises how far from Bristol these leaflets have been seen in circulation, and how few comparable productions there are. There is surely everything to be said for the *local* church having its name printed on this kind of item, with an address or two to contact and so on. They are, of course not alone in running a tape library, but they encourage us to see that it is not only a great expository ministry which can usefully be put on tape. Besides plenty of exposition, there are evangelistic sermons, talks on practical themes, the story of the church, the confirmation course, whole services of worship, and sessions of teaching on the Old Testament and Reformation from Alec Motyer and Jim Packer. Just a little imagination can capture human resources from the church's locality and make them much more widely available to the sick and elderly as well as through the post; and, of course, this is also an excellent way of helping people who are shut out of church (running the creche or Pathfinders) to stay up with the fellowship in its worship and pulpit teaching. Then too there was that prayer school—6 teaching sessions and 2 periods of prayer over a Saturday and Sunday.

Facing the new pastoral position

1. St. Michael's Bramcote on the edge of Nottingham has become one of the better known pioneers of the widespread movement to involve trained lay people in the real and continuing pastoral business of a local church. In 1974 the Vicar, Jimmy Hamilton-Brown, preached three sermons on ministry today which highlighted the relationship between ordained and lay service in the church. In the first he suggested that the New Testament envisaged two complementary strands of ministry, an officially designated group such as apostles, prophets etc. now represneted by the clergy and the whole Christian fellowship deploying its gifts in service. The ordained help to link the two by preserving a balance between Word and Spirit, maturity and enthusiasm; by co-ordinating the ministry of the whole fellowship; by promoting new ideas and setting the pace; and by discerning the good from the bad. (We found ourselves wondering if someone with such a high view of the laity might not value their contribution in some of these roles!) In the second sermon he stressed that the church was a serving body which existed not only for worship and its own concerns but to be involved in the needs of the community. In the third he looked at the qualifications for being an effective layman in the broad categories of personal faith, biblical thinking and realistic action.

The point of all this was to lay a theological foundation for the broadening of pastoral responsibility as a matter of church council policy. The intention was to select people on a geographical area basis, train them and ask the Bishop to commission them, and then give them responsibility for the material and spiritual needs of the people living in their areas.

The training of the new Church Area Leaders was worked out with the help of local clergy and Peter Ashton, the Director of Pastoral Studies at St. John's College, Nottingham (which is in this parish). The outline syllabus for their evenings of training looked like this (coffee and prayer came between the two parts of each evening—and 'homework' is added in brackets):

January 20 **1** My relationship with God. **2** Job specification (What would you say?).
February 24 **1** Sharing your faith. **2** Role play. (Bible study).
March 17 **1** Visiting. **2** Practical details, needs in parish. (Visiting—reports to be written).
April 28 **1** Reporting back on needs of visits. **2** The Christian Life. (Book—write comments).
May 12 **1** Counselling. **2** The Social Services (Bible study).
June 2 **1** Baptism, Confirmation, Bereavement, Referrals. **2** Role play. (Write a confirmation syllabus, with Bible passages).

On Sunday 22 June 1975 the Bishop of Southwell commissioned eight couples as Church Area Leaders, operating in five 'reasonably self-contained areas' within the parish. Their names and addresses were naturally given in the church magazine and in a printed leaflet with photographs which was thoroughly distributed in the respective areas. In both there was a rationale for this policy written by the Vicar and an explanation of the services the area leaders would be able to provide. These included gathering a small group for encouragement and prayer, getting to know the people of the area, acting as a link between church and area and making referrals, putting people in touch with appropriate helping agencies when needs arose. The whole life and usefulness of a church has been lifted by the use of a strategic short course, a few local resources and a single theological insight (plus, in this case, the infectious enthusiasm of an irresistible extrovert).

2. St. Ebbe's Oxford found themselves faced with the loss of their 'student curate' in clergy cuts; they also knew from experience that student Christians are very effective among their own sort. So they devised a scheme by which certain graduating students might be invited to spend a further year in Oxford to be based at the church and to work among the students. Mornings would be reserved for study, and again the resources of local clergy and a theological ocllege would be available to help design studies of the Bible and related subjects for them. The church provided accommodation, expenses, and a small personal allowance of £3 per week. They attended staff and P.C.C. meetings and spent their time otherwise with people, in home groups, families and individual contacts among the student body. Apart from the value of the scheme to them, they contributed effectively to the church's work as a whole and had the two particular good effects of feeding pastoral contacts on to the clergy for further attention, and of bridging the gap between student Christians and ordinary Christian homes. With the well-known fall-out rate among 'C.U. Christians' after they leave college, this 'earthing' process may be vital to many of their futures. Something similar is now being tried in various centres, with varying degrees of success, and it may well be a pattern for the future in training young workers as well as strengthening the arm of the churches.

3. Wandsworth Deanery is in one of those areas feeling the pinch on manpower acutely and trying to face it positively. We were sent, very kindly, an outline scheme by Mr. Mark Brickall which is receiving very serious attention in the area as a way of training ordinary church members to carry the load. We quote extensively because it speaks for itself authentically out of a grass-roots situation.

THE MINISTRY IN WANDSWORTH IN 1980

Q1. A NEW INITIATIVE REQUIRED

(1) The June 1975 Diocesan Report 'Towards Shared Ministry' recommended (like many other reports before it) 'a major expansion of lay training at every level', without spelling out what this should mean, nor who should initiate it.

(2) We are facing the prospect of having 24% fewer full-time ordained men in the Deanery in 1980 than we had in 1974. Most of our clergy are already more fully-stretched—the coming reduction will create an unbearable strain, even if we only want to maintain the existing volume of work in our churches.

(3) But we cannot be satisfied with what is going on now: there is much visiting, training, counselling, organising, etc. that is simply not getting done, because the 'ministry-team' (clergy or lay) in our parishes is not strong enough: there is little visible advance in evangelism and in service to the community. We need to *increase* our 'ministry-teams'; but we are facing a *decrease* in their full-time members.

(4) It is generally agreed that it takes 5 or 6 trained part-time workers to achieve the same volume as one full-timer. This means that as we are to lose 10 full-time clergy by 1980, we shall need 50 trained part-timers, simply to maintain the 'ministry-team' at the present strength. If we want to expand our work and witness, we shall need to double or treble that number.

(5) Rather than wait any longer for agreement on new forms of auxiliary ministry, or for official progress towards 'local elders' on 'non-stipendiary priests' (which most people know very little about) we ought to concentrate on getting more Readers (of whom we have 13 at present, and who are already recognised in all the churches) and on SPAs (Southwark Parish Auxiliaries) (of whom several of our parishes already have favourable experience).

(6) IT IS THEREFORE PROPOSED that the Deanery should set up its own training programme, starting in October 1976, with the target of calling and training 100 new Readers/SPAs for service in the Deanery by 1980.

2. THE TRAINING PROGRAMME

[*Proposals without syllabus for a basic pattern of two or three years of two lectures an evening for one night a week.*]

3. THE RESULTS IN ACTION

(1) In 1974, the average parish had two clergy and one Reader. By 1980, very few parishes will have more than one clergyman. If this scheme is carried through, the average parish would instead have a 'ministry-team' centred on one clergyman, four or five Readers, two or three SPAs, plus a good number of other lay-people trained or partly trained through these classes, and more capable of/more confident at such tasks as leading house groups, visiting, counselling, etc. than they are at present.

(2) There would be many practical advantages of having a team of this kind in every parish.

(i) Many of the well known disadvantages of the 'one-man ministry' would be eliminated, such as:
—overwork, because everyone's problem lands on the Vicar's lap.
—bearing all the burdens leading to isolation from many of the people.
—the traditional placing of the Vicar, alone, on a pedestal.
—the widespread expectation that he will exercise ALL the gifts (some of which he may not possess).
—the hiatus caused by an interregnum would be greatly reduced.

(ii) If it was *seen* that a wider group was really being expected to share deeply and officially in witnessing, service, teaching and pastoral work, it would be easier to discern, develop and utilise such gifts within the congregation. (This does sound a bit Irish, I know!).

(3) The team would clearly contain a variety of gifts:
—some, but not all, would share in preaching and teaching.
—some (not necessarily the same ones) would share in the conduct of worship.
—some might concentrate on youth work/Sunday School oversight, etc.
—some (not necessarily all) would share in pastoral work in a wide variety of different ways: one or two perhaps in preparation classes for baptism/confirmation/weddings; one or two in counselling; some in hospital work, or home visiting, or in leading a house church.

(4) It would be very natural for a team of this kind to be recognised as *de facto* 'local elders', functioning as a team very much in accordance with the sort of background which the New Testament appears to indicate, that is, of a group of elders within each individual congregation.

4. THE SCRIPTURAL BACKGROUND

[*General scriptural principles about ministers and ministry.*]

5. LIMITED OBJECTIVES ARE NECESSARY

[*Initial emphasis should be on training for ministry in local congregations.*]

February 1976

Catering for city centres

1. The London School of Christian Studies was a response to a different kind of city-centre need from that of Wandsworth. In many cities there is an eclectic group of Christians who, besides their church commitment, could well take a slightly more solid study of their faith than the individual church is geared to provide. SOCS was designed to try and meet this need in London, where it was thought the catchment area would be sufficiently large to justify drawing in visiting speakers with an expertise in ethics, church history or biblical studies beyond that of the staffs of the churches themselves. The School was launched in 1972 by All Souls, Langham Place and St. Helen's, Bishopsgate on a three-year cycle. Around 200 have been attending on Monday evenings; there are two (lecture) sessions per night with a meal between. The precise pattern has differed a little from time to time, and has recently (with mixed results) drawn in Professor Norman Anderson's London Lectures in Contemporary Ethics. They comment, 'The syllabus is straightforward and effectiveness depends on the speaker! . . . Note absence of teaching or training in pastoral work . . . No formal integration into church programme . . . Confined to study.'

THE SCHOOL OF CHRISTIAN STUDIES 3 YEAR CYCLE

Autumn 72	**1.** What Christians believe about God	J. I. Packer
	What Christians believe about Man	H. Silvester
	2. Christian Behaviour and Contemporary Moral Issues	D. Field
Spring 73	**1.** Authority	J. R. W. Stott
	2. The Reformation and its personalities	P. Dawes
Autumn 73	**1.** The Person and Work of Christ	H. Silvester
	2. Contemporary Challenges to the Gospel	J. W. Charley
	Communism	M. Goldsmith
	Humanism	T. Kitwood
	Mysticism	J. Wesson
Spring 74	**1.** Introduction to the Old Testament:	
	The Old Testament and its teaching	J. B. Taylor
	The Old Testament and its problems	J. A. Motyer
	2. Men and Movements in Modern Church History (various speakers): The Evangelical Revival—The Clapham Sect: Evangelicals and Social Reform—The Oxford Movement—Liberalism: 'Darwin and All That'—The Missionary Movement—Evangelism since Moody—Evangelicals and the Ecumenical Movement.	
Autumn 74	**1.** The Outpoured Spirit—Lord and Lifegiver:	R. C. Lucas
	The Old Testament Background—Christ and the Spirit—Baptism and the Spirit—Truth and the Spirit—The Church and the Spirit—Holiness and the Spirit—Revival and the Spirit.	
	2. Early Church History (various speakers): The Emergence of the Church—Heresies and the Defence of the Faith—Church and State—Battles for Truth—The Rise of the Christian Faith in Britain—Spiritual Life in Mediaeval Britain.	
Spring 75	**1.** Jesus and the New Testament:	C. Byworth
	The Historical Backcolth—The Synoptic Gospels—The Gospel of John—Paul—The Message of Paul—The Gospel Confronts Contemporary Culture—The Book of Revelation.	
	2. Some Challenges Facing the Church (various speakers): The Doctrine of the Church—The World Church To-day—The Church and Urban Society—The Church and New Theology—The Church and Revolution—The Church and People.	

2. Care and Counsel may be part of London's answer on the question of pastoral care. There has of course been an increasing need for the churches to be able to cope a little more deeply with some of the emotional ,stress, personality and relationship problems which our present society is throwing up. In some of the large cities this has reached almost epidemic proportions and most Christians, ministers included, flet ill equipped to do much to help. It was another area of training crying out for attention. In setting up Care and Counsel several London churches hope that this will be an agency for training as well as eventually providing some direct counselling services for when the churches get out of their depth. It may well be something that other parts of the country can use and emulate in due course. The aims of the service bear so much on a quite fresh area of training that they should be quoted in part:

(a) Caring We cherish the vision of each Christian congregation as a caring, welcoming community, and we hope to offer help towards the deepening of fellowship and amturing of relationships throughout the local church. We envisage the development within each of a caring group who accept responsibility to give support to people with problems and to those going through a period of stress. *Care and Counsel* will offer support to these groups by consultation, advice, and encouragement. It has also completed its first seminar for clergy . . .

(b) Educating We are strong believers in the need to promote community health and human maturity. So we plan an educational programme which will include regular group courses

(i) for young people on growth, sex, love, courtship, engagement and marriage

(ii) for engaged couples on marriage

(iii) for married couples on their mauring relationship and the implications of parenthood.

In addition a first series of public lectures has been given on the major crises of life (adolescence, marriage, parenthood, the middle years, bereavement and death). Against the background of widening divergence between Christian and non-Christian concepts of sexual behaviour, marriage and the family, we shall seek to commend the Christian understanding of these important areas of life.

(c) Counselling A personal counselling service by professionally qualified people will also be offered . . .

(Further information: *Care and Counsel,* 2 All Souls Place, London W1N 3DB).

3. Birmingham Cathedral and the Jesus Centre overlap in their teaching efforts to some extent, at least in personnel (teachers and learners). Here the problem of the city centre can be tackled from both ends, in providing a major forum for midday meetings in the week together with the more intimate environment for personal discussion and group work. David MacInnes reports that three lunchtimes are now used: 'On Tuesday: 25 minutes of teaching, evangelism usually exposition. On Wednesday: we are starting a once monthly evangelistic occasion with the other 3 or 4 lunch-hours used for basic Christian teaching . . . Thursdays have been used for taking sections of the Bible, both Old Testament and New for expository teaching for Christians of some experience. We do sometimes turn these into subjects . . . at other times we have had courses in the lunch hour for about 8 weeks for clergy and Christian leaders on subjects related to the Charismatic Renewal, the Holy Spirit, healing and so on. We have also had series of training sessions for young people who are potential leaders. We have also had one or two courses on relationships and helping young people to develop self-awareness.' Quite a mixture! The worship and praise event known as Youthquake has also contained teaching.

At the Jesus Centre a course of basic Christian teaching and its relation to social questions has been worked out, but has not yet been fully tried. Here follows an outline of the syllabus together with some teaching material.

BASIC CHRISTIAN TEACHING [headings only are given here]

1	The Gospel	**9**	Healing
2	The Church	**10**	Spiritual Warfare
3	The Normal Christian	**11**	Prayer
4	The Work of the Spirit	**12**	Ministries in the Church
5	Practical Evangelism	**13**	An Introduction to the Bible
6	The Christian Community	**14**	Relationships
7	The History of the Church	**15**	Meditation Series
8	What Shall I Do?	**16**	Expositions of Books of the Bible

SOCIAL QUESTIONS

1. *THE CHRISTIAN ATTITUDE TO:* Pornography—Abortion—Homosexuality—Vandalism—War—Demonstrations—Censorship.
2. *CHRISTIANITY AND . . .* Science—Economics—Politics—Race Relations—Trades Unions—Business Management—The Press—Radio and TV.
3. *HOW A CITY IS ORGANIZED:* The Council—Power Structures—Housing—Roads—Youth—Old people—Education—The Arts—Health and medicine—Commerce—Social services.
4. *THE CHRISTIAN CHURCH OVERSEAS:* In North America—In Europe—In the Warsaw Pact countries—In the Middle East—In South America—In Africa—In India—In S.E. Asia—In China.
5. *INTERNATIONAL PROBLEMS:* The pollution problem—The population problem—The economic problem.
6. *PSYCHOLOGY AND CHRISTIANITY:* Understanding myself—Depression—Fear—Anxiety—Recognizing mental illness—Counselling others—Guilt—Loneliness—Boredom.
7. *WHAT THEY BELIEVE:* Introduction to Jehovah's Witnesses—Mormons—Christian Science—Christadelphians—7th Day Adventists—Marxism—Humanism—Freemasonry—Jews—Hindus—Muslims—Sikhs—Buddhists—Shintoists—Animists—Hare Krishna—Divine Light Mission—Scientology—Unified Family—Children of God.
8. *CHRISTIANITY AND THE ARTS:* Music—Drama—Poetry.

RELATIONSHIPS ANALYSIS [Part of hand-out material provided]

Requirements in relationships
(Roles)

Acceptance/Status, Protection, Love, Encouragement, Freedom, Forgiveness, Sharing/Trust, Honesty, Explanations, Growth, Companionship

Difficulties in relationships
(Role uncertainty)
(Role perversion)

—What is expected of those involved in the relationship?

Unacceptance, Discouragement, Restrictiveness, Unforgiveness, Mistrust/Fear, Dishonesty

Answers to difficulties

(1) Establish what each person is wanting out of the relationship.
(2) Acknowledge the situation as it exists.
(3) Determine the agreed potential for the relationship.
(4) ACT ON IT!

QUOTE!! 'I am not in this world to live up to your expectations, and you are not in this world to live up to my expectations, I am I, and you are you, and when we meet it's beautiful.'

4. THE FUTURE

For the present, several broad trends emerge. Most sweeping is that many churches are giving the training of their members, under various guises, a priority which it has not enjoyed for many years. In particular this shows up in the training for mutual care and prayer in the small group and in the service-orientated training of courses in evangelism, Bible study leading, and the like. Training towards various species of pastoral responsibility has been one of the healthiest responses to the present crisis in clergy manpower, as churches train group leaders, area representatives, Readers and elders. Although the churches surveyed were probably far from typical, we hear enough from our own areas and the church press to gain the impression that similar needs are giving birth to similar expedients in other places. If these churches happen to be out in front, they are all the more helpful to stimulate others into action and give some material to chew on. One church which runs no regular scheme beyond confirmation classes and home groups noted: 'Before a recent mission which we as a parish took in another parish, we had a three month course of preparation in in Christian doctrine . . . The fact that about 120 attended this every week, shows perhaps the need and desire for such courses.' It is the need and desire which have come together, and which we are obliged to try to meet.

For the future, the place is littered with question-marks. The Church of England as a whole is far from deciding by what means it hopes to meet the ministry needs not covered by future clergy. It will probably not do so until it has clarified its theology of ministry, which has vitiated discussions on women's ordination, plans for Auxiliary Pastoral Ministry, and a dozen other issues. For the meanwhile the initiative will lie locally and will have to go for *ad hoc* plans of the vision and practicality of Wandsworth's or Bramcote's. Christians with gifts to deploy are finding the confidence to use them and the realism to discard the myth of the Vicar's omnicompe-petence. What they should also be finding is that part of the vicar's com-pretence is the ability to give, or at least to lay on, a kind of training which will sharpen and liberate further the gifts which Christians have to offer.

One question mark will concern the resources upon which that Vicar can draw. One noticeable feature of the schemes described above was the progress made by those within reach of a theological college, where a good brain and a spare pair of hands has often been available to service local ideas into reality: it is true of Bramcote, SOCS, Clifton and Pip 'n' Jay, as well as a scheme at St Aldate's alongside that of St. Ebbe's in Oxford. The Bishops are working on a suggestion that there be ten theological 'centres' for future clergy training which will draw on the resources of cathedrals, universities, polytechnics and colleges of education as well as existing theological colleges. That is fine (some would feel wildly overdue) —but what about the availability of those same resources to the training of the church at large ? We cannot put it better than the Education Secretary of SAMS, Eddie Gibbs, speaking recently about the situation in South America: 'However brilliant our training for ordination may be, it gives the impression *to the local church* that the *real* training for ministry happens elsewhere than here.' We need to rehabilitate the view that real, normal

Christian training happens in the local church (and may, where essential, be supplemented by specialist training elsewhere). In this process the theological colleges have already shown themselves very willing to take a part by their support of church training schemes wherever they can. But this area, and not only that of clergy training, must be part of the debate about the colleges' future; and the question of other resources, in cathedrals, universities etc., should be asked urgently in terms of their helpfulness to local churches in equipping their Christians for the work of ministry.

As for the local church, its future plans of course depend on its situation. But basically most churches have more resources around than they realise, especially if they will look around their deanery and the academic and practical competence of their local clergy and church members. The deanery of Chelsea, for instance (not as untypical as it sounds) has at least four churches trying to do fairly ambitious things in the training field, yet with little co-ordination; one of the best signs is the way in which the Rural Dean has systematically formed the Chapter meeting into (primarily) a study group. With a little thought, the potential is often there. The kite flown in the meeting from which this booklet took flight is worth another look. If some central body drew up an outline syllabus which local churches or groups of churches could follow with the use of local teachers and resources, would this help? Who should do it? Would there be any value in a national certificating scheme, especially given the mobility of our society (and in particular our middle-class church members)? Readers and A.P.M.-ers are, of course, the product of that kind of vision, but they are only a beginning in terms of the needs and the potential.

Children will remain a bone of contention, and much will depend on the direction taken by the national educational system. On the one hand we probably still need to come to terms with a reduction in the amount of background Christian knowledge children will acquire at school, and we should be making provision to fill the gap. On the other there seems to be a growing recognition that the churches have in the past poured resources into young people's work which has neither yielded a proportionate return nor taken seriously enough the need for manpower for adult work. In some ways this survey has shown up the way in which adult evangelism and whole-family work are coming to life, and redressing the balance.

It would be sad to leave in mind the vision of a church training members to meet a decline in full-time workers. We are, instead, training members for a new situation in the world church, where a new hunger for Christian truth and a fresh desire for Christian growth are evident. Our training ought not to be a defensive reaction to local needs but a positive means of fulfilling faithfully the commission which God has laid upon us. Compare our own commitment with an old but apposite entry in *Encyclopaedia Britannica:*

'Throughout the Soviet Union there are 6,000 special schools maintained by the Party and devoted exclusively to training professional propagandists. These have an enrolment at any one time of 185,000 students. Above these schools are 177 Regional Propaganda Colleges to train 135,000 alumni of the local schools. And above the regional schools are a dozen higher institutions giving "graduate training" to several thousand advanced students. Propaganda is by far the biggest industry in the U.S.S.R.'